CHEAT THE CHEATER

DISCOVERING THE LOVING CHEAT

SOLOMON M. U

Copyright © 2020 SOLOMON M. U

All Rights Reserved

TABLE OF CONTENTS

INTRODUCTION

When you fall in love with someone you automatically drop down most of your guilds. You see yourself doing things others will call "you being crazy", but the good part of the whole analyses, is that the someone in love will not even care what anyone say about their partner.

Sadly, most people find themselves in an unsuitable relationship where they will be the one doing all the loving while the other partner will be busy doing the opposite.

Some great minds find themselves in a toxic relationship, they might eventually discover the hidden truth about their partner's unfaithfulness, to tell you the truth, this is a very difficult state to be.

Some great minds even go so low, they find themselves engaging in physical combat with someone they once love, some even go down to the earth by committing suicide.

This book was written to help the faithful lovers discover a cheating partner before things get out of hands, as this will give them the opportunity and choice to make their choices on time.

I am not a fan of broken relationship, however, I am a great fan of breaking a toxic relationship.

Click on purchase now to read more, or read more on Amazon kindle unlimited.

CHAPTER ONE

SIGNS YOUR SPOUSE COULD BE CHEATING

Unfaithfulness is one of all the more testing issues glanced in a relationship. While various people are sucker-punched if and when they find a few solutions concerning a friend or lover cheating, others may relate it considering the way that with exercises that are odd.

While everyone is one of a kind, and very few signs of cheating are finished, there are certain practices that, together, may back up your pitiful hunch.

Expected Signs of Infidelity

Direct changes, curious exercises, and odd occasions can without a doubt show that an accessory is taking part in extramarital relations. Taking everything into account, review that that isn't commonly the circumstance.

If you estimate that your lover is cheating, it is sensible to require a total technique to show your uncertainty. While things like wandering outside to talk on the phone could be related to selling out, there may be various explanations.

Consider the potential signs that your lover isn't being dedicated to. As ought to be self-evident, a part of these signs truly is at chances with one another. This extent of possible results, which is verifiably not exhaustive of everything, gives precisely how different signs can be beginning with one individual then onto the following.

Changes in Your Sex Life

It isn't momentous for there to be changes in the repeat of sex in your marriage. Regardless, these signs may show the opportunity of an issue. There is widely less closeness or relationship in your relationship. How about checking your sex life with these signals.

Your sexual concurrence is in every practical sense non-existent.

There are loads of new things introduced in sex that were at no other time.

You find that you have an STD and you have not meandered.

Sudden Change in Habits.

Your lover may change their affinities for a combination of reasons. Besides, solid affinity changes are commonly a positive thing. Nevertheless, certain inclination changes may be cause for concern.

The words "I love you" are not spoken by your life accomplice any longer.

You can't get your ally to talk with you (stonewalling).

Your partner is unexpectedly more careful than anticipated.

Your partner seems to require risk or energizes in his/her life.

Your partner is dressing more wonderful, looking more charming, or there is a sudden excitement for appearance.

Your partner gets another side interest that requires several significant lots of duty consistently. Exactly when you show an eagerness for their new preoccupation, their answer gives off an impression of being dark or they excuse you.

Your mate's wandering eye has all the earmarks of being wild.

Mentality Changes.

He or she may encounter work pressure or issues with different connections that can prompt changes in mentality. At the point when you see these signs think about different causes, just as the potential for unfaithfulness.

Your lover displays indications of low confidence.

You notice your that he or she has a feeling of disarray about oneself.

Your lover is more negative than previously.

They turn out to be more condemning of you.

Your lover is by all accounts starting quarrel all the more frequently.

Your companion gets exceptionally cautious in the event that you notice disloyalty or undertakings.

Your life partner appears to be more mysterious.

Your lover deserts strict confidence.

Lack of interest.

At the point when your life partner shows detachment or absence of enthusiasm for things that they used to adore, speak with them to check whether there is another explanation behind the adjustment in commitment.

Be that as it may, in the event that you additionally speculate treachery these progressions might be a further sign of an undertaking.

Your friend gives off an impression of being depleted with you, work, your youths, redirections, or even life all things considered.

Your friend has gotten drowsy, especially around the house.

Your friend doesn't show any longing about you, paying little mind to what you state.

Your partner is indifferent to family events like birthday festivities and events.

Money Issues.

Basically, all connections experience a type of budgetary concern on the double or another. In any case, you may need to inspect certain money issues when you notice them in your marriage.

You notice charges on budgetary records that don't look good.

Money ends up being a more prominent measure of an issue among you.

They stop making plans for colossal purchases, (for instance, a trip, buying a house, starting an upgrade, etc.)

A change in technology use.

Injustice is normally revealed on the web, in texts, or phone messages. These tech changes may warrant concern.

You notice cloud sharing has out of the blue been killed on your contraptions.

Your partner stops using shared contraptions all around.

Your partner reduces their usage of online media.

Your lover clears the program history on the home PC.

Your friend's wellbeing tracker shows practice on odd events and hours.

Again, what may be an advice sign in one relationship maybe not something to be stressed over in another relationship.

Surely, most signs of traitorousness are honest. It is exactly when the misrepresentations and stories quit including that the cheating typically gets noticeable.

You should be able to pick these points and try to talk things with your lover, eventually they will often tell you that all is well and that he or she is just going through a process that they can handle. But I tell you they are playing tricks on you, you should be mindful of these move I warn you.

CHAPTER TWO

UNCOVERING A CHEATING PARTNER

Consider how conceivable it is that they deny it. By what means will things change? If you expect your buddy is assaulting you or even a little degree undermining you, you have a lot to consider.

Notwithstanding, before you approach them, spin around a part of these woeful signs that they might be cheating. Here are some clear signs that most person miss

Wearing new or various pieces of clothing

In case your shirt and jeans ornamentation surprisingly start wearing lavish or by and large extraordinary pieces of clothing, or if they are just getting into clean pieces of clothing occurring to wearing their upheld position shirt for a really noteworthy time period, something presumably won't be right.

If your adornment has had a close to hairdo for a long time yet all of a sudden has a striking new hairstyle. If they are unexpectedly tidying up for an indispensable night, contributing essentialness with new people, and getting back home at the whole hours of the night without explanation, you might be in an irritating condition.

On the occasion that they're abstaining from reacting to your requesting or if you notice their story is changing as much as their garments these days, something might be changing for them that leave you contemplating what the heck happened among you.

When associates are cheating, they will unmistakably change the way wherein they present themselves to the world since they have to appear, apparently, to be addressing someone else.

They are concealing things from you on their telephone.

On the off chance that they appear to freeze when you get their telephone or PC and are unexpectedly attempting to control what you may or may not be able to on their telephone, something isn't right, it is not that romantic when you feel your partner is hiding something from you, concealing things from you on their telephone might be an indication of cheating:

They could be attempting to abstain from accepting any sketchy calls or messages.

In the event that you notice that your accomplice is erasing writings and continually clearing their perusing history, at that point that may not be a decent sign.

You can't discover them or contact them

Couples that have been together for some time will in general know each other's timetable. On the off chance that the individual isn't where they should be, or on the off chance that they are not doing what they reveal to you they are doing, it may be an ideal opportunity to plunk down and ask them what is happening.

At the point when individuals are misleading about their whereabouts or rationalize why plans changed, things aren't acceptable. In the event that you can't discover them or contact them, there may be a purpose behind that and this is on the grounds that they don't need you to comprehend why.

Feeling unessential

A sign that a man is undermining a lady is the point at which he begins to feel unessential to her.

For a man, feeling basic to a lady is frequently what isolates "like" from "adoration". What's more, feeling unessential is a typical trigger for pulling ceaselessly and investigating their alternatives somewhere else.

Try not to misunderstand me, presumably your person cherishes your quality and capacities to be autonomous. Be that as it may, he despite everything and he needs to feel needed and valuable not unimportant!

This is because men have a fundamental need for something "more vital" that goes past friendship or sex. It's the explanation men who evidently have the "perfect darling" are so far upset and wrap up constantly searching for something else, or to finish everything off.

Fundamentally, men have a characteristic drive to feel required, to feel critical, and to oblige the woman he contemplates.

Male needs are not confounded, essentially misinterpreted. Motivations are unfathomable drivers of human direct and this is especially legitimate for how men approach their associations.

Hence, when the holy person instinct isn't set off, men are most likely not going to zero in on a relationship with any woman. He holds down considering the way he views her; this is essential because he build the relationship around what he holds down in his heart.

In addition, he won't totally open to you aside from on the off chance that you give him a sentiment of significance reason and cause him to feel as the like the key to your unlocked doors.

In a genuine way, you basically need to show your man what you require and grant him to step up to fulfill it.

By setting off this amazingly trademark male instinct, you'll give him more significant satisfaction just as help to rocket your relationship to the accompanying level.

There's no closeness.

If it's been three months since you've moved around in the roughage, something is being done the wrong way you need to up your game.

Recollect that couples create through dry spells, anyway if the individual isn't regardless, showing energy for you and nothing has really happened to cause the partition between you, cheating might be an inspiration driving.

They is no time, you needn't waste time with anything, since they are having their necessities satisfied by someone else.

They are irritated and anxious around you

On the off chance that your benevolent partner is

abruptly irate and baffled with you, realize that it's presumably not you, then they are dissatisfied with life around you, they might think and feel that are having a better opportunity with the other partner that are flexing with outside.

It's not generally apparent in light of the fact that a few people change after some time. Not every person is who they initially had all the earmarks of being and it occurs occasionally that one accomplice discovers the other accomplice isn't who they said they were.

In any case, on the off chance that they have been a major part of your life for quite a while and are getting distraught at you for things that don't bode well, it could be concealment.

you can tell if your accomplice is concealing something on the off chance that "they are shaking to and fro" when they are visiting with you. This gives an indication of apprehension.

Their timetable is unexpectedly extraordinary

In the event that they need to take off for a couple of days for work and no, you can't go as well, something may not be right.

In the event that you've generally voyaged together and now they are stating you can't come, cheating may be the reason.

On the off chance that the person is going with a work partner and have a lot of work gatherings and you are not allowed to go in view of "organization governs", there's no organization on the planet that would state that.

Who has the privilege to prevent you from following along, particularly on the off chance that you are taking care of yourself? No one. It's fishy.

In case you're seeing this side effect, just as a portion of the others, it doesn't really mean your accomplice is cheating. Notwithstanding, you do need to begin making a move to stop the corruption in your relationship.

Companions being bizarre

On the off chance that you can't discover any proof of cheating however you are sure something isn't right, then something might be not as it seems with his companions, probably he is with another partner that knows you, the other person your partner might be cheating with knows you and he or she is strictly playing along with the perfect game.

In the event that their companions can't look at you without flinching or are being odd about it, something's incorrect. It's a surefire approach to tell if your accomplice is cheating.

All of a sudden, they are giving a lot of thought to you in the wake of being unavailable for quite a while

They may be endeavoring to make up for not actually ideal acts notwithstanding your great confidence. If you find they are making a respectable endeavor when they're around you, it might be an ideal chance to have a conversation about where the sudden thought is beginning. Is your man pulling unendingly?

Make an effort not to submit this one BIG mistake.

They are all of a sudden testy without explanation or propitiatory supposition.

On the occasion that they're disguising something, they likely won't cover it quite well.

At times, people are genuinely out and out horrible remaining prudent concealed and they'll endeavor to nail a lot of fault to you and point out all the things you are messing up to eliminate the light from them.

It's a control system that endeavors to cause you to appear like the miscreant so you won't be surprised when you find that she/he was subverting you.

Regardless, note that they may basically be having a horrible day, yet in case you can't find any clarification behind their sudden change in feeling, by then it might be an ideal chance to start thinking.

They are not excited about the things they used to be enthusiastic about

If they're not enthusiastic about going to clubs or embarking to your friends' homes or they're not wanting to go out using any and all means, something may not be correct.

Right when models and inclinations change, there is typically a tolerable explanation for it. Notwithstanding the way that it most likely won't be an explanation, you have to hear.

If you are focused on that things are going south and that they most likely won't be enthusiastic about you any more, demand a genuine conversation about where things are going.

They are not irritated by things that used to make them crazy

Another way to deal with telling if they might be subverting you is if they quit denouncing you to pound all your sad inclinations.

If they used to be aggravated by your loud eating uproars or your plates on the counter, it might be in light of the fact that they have stopped pondering the relationship or they see a leave plan.

Exactly when that is the circumstance, they'll quit exaggerating things since they no longer need you to change. That might be because they've found someone who is starting at now not doing those things.

Significantly less or more sex in the relationship

Both decreased and extended degrees of sexual development are something to pay special mind to.

Both diminished and expanded degrees of sexual development in your relationship can be an indication of irresoluteness. Less sex happens considering how your partner is spun around another person; more sex happens on the grounds that they are attempting to cover that up.

They may not require as much sex as they used to in case they're being satisfied by someone else. Or on the other hand possibly the volume of sex is the identical, yet there is apparently a nonappearance of excited affiliation.

Or then again, they have an extended sex drive since they feel remorseful about their issue and they're endeavoring to cover it up.

They're remaining in contact

In case they're going to rest early or later or getting up without contact, or if they are not sitting on the parlor seat when they all around plunk down near you, something's going on.

There's no clarification for them to avoid being around you other than that it causes them pulverized or makes them feel to blame.

If that is the condition, your most sharpened decision is to sit them down and have a conversation about what's going on so you can both make decisions about the predetermination of your relationship together.

They are zeroing in on their appearance more than predicted

In case your extra is finding a wide degree of better ways to deal with oversee manage to show up in style, it may be a sign that they are endeavoring to catch the eye of someone else or, in case you are looking for the positive side to all the focusing in on that keeps you mindful around night, consider that they should look through bravo.

If that doesn't seem to concur with you and you are sure that something more toxic is going on, by then

seeing how they plan and how they dress contrastingly might be the focal sign you need to get something going.

You aren't sure what they are up to constantly

If you used to know where your lover hung out or who they were going to dinner with before things seemed to change, it might legitimize zeroing in on.

Punctured tires, dead batteries, gridlocks, investing additional energy at the exercise center, and comparable reasons for being late or missing out and out might likewise flag disloyalty."

Remember that individuals' timetables change, yet in the event that you are not having a nice sentiment

about such changes, the best game-plan is to address your accomplice about your interests.

They assault you for immaterial things

It may be unsettling to find that your accomplice is pulling endlessly from you, however, it doesn't imply that everything is lost. Here and there, individuals experience difficult stretches and they need their space.

However, more often than not, we're entirely acceptable at perceiving when something is happening. The human body is astounding in its ability for observing reality in others.

What is alarming, nonetheless, is the point at which

that space gets littler and your accomplice begins to

upbraid you for things they never thought about.

For instance, your accomplice may shout and shout about how you did the dishes toward the end of the week or how you left a messy dish on the counter as opposed to clearing it off.

While great housekeeping may recommend that you wash the messy dish, there's no requirement for anybody to holler and shout about it.

You sense that you are getting the brush off

With regard to connections, you can anticipate that they should have recurring patterns. Everybody experiences difficult stretches, however on the off chance that you are encountering one that has emerged from the blue or has appeared to be continuing for quite a while, you may be right and on track with everything you are doing, but they will always find that loose edge to complain, it will be wish to speculate things could turn sour.

Before they get excessively insane, or before you lose your direction, take your accomplice back to you with a discussion about your interests and how you need to help reinforce your relationship.

Despite how they are the ones carrying on of the standard, it's colossal that you perceive how you are acting in the relationship as well.

Tolerating a commitment for your activities can go far to enable your accomplice to see that they don't have to take off to somewhere else to get what they are searching for.

They reveal to you they won't be around for a long time

In the event that your extra is dropping encounters that they will be going withdrawn or away for whenever period and that feels unpredictable to you, it's essential that you make and present solicitations about what's happening.

Two or three people basically need their space, in any case in the event that you think it is undermining the relationship you love, talk with your colleague.

Your partner is all of a sudden getting even more unfriendly to you and the relationship

It might sound drawing in, yet cheats will when everything is said in done recognize that what they're doing is right. They maintain they're direct apparently. One standard approach to manage do this is to charge you.

They may reveal to themselves that it's alright to cheat since you don't look as unequivocally captivating as you used to, or it's the common, depleted incapacitating consideration in you in the room.

Since this gets embedded in their cerebrum, they may begin taking care of the inadequacy of you for their shiftiness. Senseless, isn't that so?

Obviously, if your partner is incredibly short with you

or upset with you, by then that is an issue of itself and you should exchange with them about it.

Unexplained costs

Seeing any odd charges on your associate's Visa?

Is there shockingly less cash in your fundamental financial equality (on the off chance that you have one)?

The truth is

Unfaithfulness costs cash. There are trips, suppers, lodgings (the rundown goes on).

The expense of cheating can include rapidly. In the event that you abruptly notice large bills from places, you don't perceive, at that point that may not be a decent sign.

They simply don't appear to be associated with you sincerely

Presently don't misunderstand me. No relationship will be as extraordinary as it was in the initial months. That is the energetic stage we've likely totally experienced.

Nonetheless, as time goes, we will in general bond and safely connect after some time, prompting more trust with one another. Enthusiastic closeness is the thing that keeps this reliable bond alive.

On the off chance that your accomplice needs to discuss this, at that point that might be a terrible sign.

Since it shows that it's something they're genuinely contemplating, or it, at any rate, shows that they're troubled in the relationship.

They moreover might be endeavoring to check your reaction in case you find they are cheating. "when cheating isn't excessively far off, every now and again hear associates list a specific kind of individual, a zone, period of the day, or they may even name someone in their life."

Your lover comes out and says that particular practices don't contain cheating

By and by it's exceptional for lovers to truly have a real conversation about what involves cheating.

Conventionally, this is something that shouldn't be examined considering the way that it's so undeniable.

Nonetheless, if you do have a conversation about swindling when everything is said in done, for instance, playing with someone else, they may vivaciously watch how it isn't cheating.

Clearly, it may be cheating, yet if they're really excited about their situation, by then it could be a sign that they're achieving something erroneously.

They by and large need to know where you'll be

Maybe they have to know how much time they have to sneak around, or potentially they're meeting their relationship in open somewhere.

Whatever it is, if your lover ceaselessly has to know where you are, it may not be too bad as you would speculate, they might just be at the starting point of whatever they are up to, and at this point things could get better if both lover could sit and talk about issues and try to remedy them right away.

They're ending up being progressively questionable

Exactly when you're single, gigantic quantities of us routinely search for endorsement from being charming to the next sexual orientation, in any case, that all leave for good when you're seeing somebody, If your lover is feeling particularly down, they may search for endorsement from various females or folks, which may incite an issue.

By and by this isn't really remarkable. We in general like recognition, nonetheless, someone that is inadequate in bravery may welcome the acclamations so much that they take it further and search after a relationship.

You can check whether their assurance is persevering through a shot if they question whether you really welcome them and whether you're genuinely pulled in to them anymore. On the occasion that they're not getting the endorsement, they need from you, by then they may search for it elsewhere.

CHAPTER THREE

DO DUPING PARTNER ACTUALLY CHANGE

This question often pop up when an individual still love his or her cheating partner, even after they have discovered and uncovered their tricks that they have been playing on their intelligence, in some cases the partner that was cheated find it extremely difficult to part ways with the cheat, thus they begin to ask the above question.

Any individual who has ever been undermined will have no issue disclosing to you that an accomplice who has cheated once will do it again.

The dread is reasonable for such individuals who have been sung once.

Also, it's much more terrible on the off chance that they excused the accomplice, just for the person in question to go out there and do it once more, again and again till every single smidgen of trust is scratched off their accomplice's spirits. Yet, that is by all accounts just an aspect of the story. Miscreants do surely change.

I know somebody who was at one time a terrible cheat, a lone ranger. At the stature of his philandering, he once bolted out his meeting sweetheart till he got done with his side chick. At the point when he was done, he put the side chick in his flat mate's room before going to open the entryway for his sweetheart who was in tears at the embarrassment. Nothing occurred and he stayed in a relationship with her for quite a while after that.

Nowadays, however, he's in another relationship and he's so dedicated to his better half. Another lady could be exposed before him and he would leave. He's that loyal.

Individuals who can't change have never felt the horrendous blame that comes when you understand you've committed an awful error by having a single night rendezvous or an issue.

Cheating truly doesn't need to be the grounding of a relationship.

The genuine danger of losing a relationship they worth could instruct individuals to wake up and act right if their accomplice would have them back.

Remember, cheating shouldn't be the grounding of a relationship. It could excite lovers to prize and clutch their relationship more tightly than any time in recent memory.

It is an incorrect method to manage relationship clashes, however at the nadir of uncertain relationship issues and disengagement from their lover, individuals have been known to get stirred up in things they shouldn't do.

CHAPTER FOUR

COMMON MARRIAGE PROBLEMS AND SOLUTIONS

B it by bit guidelines to Deal With a Lying Spouse

All around, regardless, when you face it you unite as one with charges of cheating, it will be denied. But on the off chance that you have hard evidence or obvious check, many won't admit to disloyalty.

There are two or three different ways that you can tell if your mate is lying. In case you keep getting refusal and push-back when endeavoring to discuss your

inclinations with your associate, you may need to get capable help to make sense of things.

Tips on how to handle a cheating partner

Discovering that your accomplice has been faithless can hit you like a huge amount of blocks. Your marriage might be tossed into a condition of emergency that may annihilate it.

It is normal to need to know why your accomplice cheated, yet there is seldom a basic response to why somebody gets untrustworthy. It could be an indication of different issues in your marriage, it could identify with something in your accomplice's past, or it could be absolutely disconnected to you or to your marriage.

Regardless of the reason, you'll have a ton of muddled emotions to figure out, and a great deal to consider as you conclude how to push ahead.

These eight hints can assist you in adapting to the consequence of treachery:

Acknowledge Your Feelings

Stun, tumult, dread, agony, despondency, and disarray are ordinary. You will probably feel like you're on a passionate rollercoaster for a while.

It requires some investment to get past the agony of having an untrustworthy mate. Try not to expect the blend of sentiments and the question to disappear regardless of whether you're attempting to excuse your accomplice and fix your marriage. Your marriage has changed and it is normal to lament the relationship you once had.

Try not to Seek Revenge

Being double-crossed by your accomplice can incite rage. In your incensed express, your first nature might be to rebuff your mate by garbage talking him to companions (or more awful, via web-based media), or consider having an unsanctioned romance yourself to settle the score.

You may get an impermanent feeling of fulfillment from such activities, at the end of the day they can neutralize you, keeping you in a condition of outrage as opposed to zeroing in on recuperating and proceeding onward, alone or together.

Think before you tell your family, also. They will probably have solid sentiments about what you ought to do leave or remain. Yet, no one else truly comprehends what goes on in someone else's marriage. While you are contemplating how you will continue, it's ideal to keep the subtleties hidden.

Attempt to Take Care of Yourself

You may have some physical responses because of stress, for example, queasiness, loose bowels, rest issues (excessively little or to an extreme), flimsiness, trouble concentrating, not having any desire to eat, or indulging.

When the underlying stun has passed, make an honest effort to eat well nourishments, to remain on a timetable, to rest ordinary hours, to get some activity every day, to drink a lot of water, and, truly, to have a great time.

Dodge the Blame Game

Accusing yourself, your accomplice, or the outsider won't transform anything and its simply squandered vitality. Make an effort not to play the person in question, either, on the off chance that you can support it, or flounder in self-indulgence. It will just cause you to feel more powerless and terrible about yourself.

Keep Your Kids out of It

This circumstance is among you and your accomplice and ought not include your youngsters. Regardless of whether you have chosen to end your marriage, sharing insights concerning an issue will just place your children in an illogical position, causing them uneasiness, causing them to feel stuck in the center, and compelled to favor one side.

Quest for Counseling

Take the necessary steps not to try to move past changing in accordance with faltering alone. Before you settle on any choices about whether to end your marriage, it's wise to converse with a couple's mentor, who will be unbiased and can assist you with getting data into what effectively happened. You can ask your partner demands and offer your assessments without losing your cool.

A rehearsed ace can assist you with passing on better and cycle finishes of the flaw, disgrace, and whatever else you may be feeling. In the event that you choose to end the marriage, you'll comprehend that you set forth an authentic endeavor to make it work.

On the off chance that you accept that the undertaking will probably incite the finishing of your marriage, consider to reasonable issues, for example, where you will live, on the off chance that you have enough cash to pay for your nuts and bolts, and, in the event that you have youths, such a thoughtful arrangement you need.

You may in like way need to believe advancing toward your lover to be sought after for STDs and to get yourself endeavored moreover on the off chance that you have had intercourse during or after the issue.

Take It One Day right away

Shamefulness is one of the more badly designed difficulties a marriage can challenge, in any case, it doesn't regularly mean it's the end. As you work through the result after some time, it will wind up being away from to continue so going with a great time, together or detached, can start.

CHAPTER FIVE

DREAMS AS A CHEATING SIGNAL

Interestingly, while there might be an opportunity it's a mystic hunch (in the event that you have faith in that), your tricking dream is doubtlessly not exacting. Proposes inquiring as to whether you have the motivation to speculate your accomplice's cheating. In the event that you don't, odds are they're most certainly not. Here are a couple of things that fantasy about your accomplice cheating could mean.

What do dreams about your associate misleading mean? It's fundamental to separate who they're cheating with.

You're Scared They'll Cheat

Those with ceaseless conning dreams may feel questionable about their own charm and fear their lover will find someone better. If this is something you worry over customarily during the day, it looks good that your advantages will find their way into your dreams around night time.

Whatever the wellspring of the fear, the dream may show a certified fear that you could benefit by discussing with your lover. It is hard to yield frailties, extensively less conversation about cheating. In any case, if you can move it out from the shadows and let your associate acknowledge how you've been feeling, it could achieve more trust and sponsorship and scarcely any less cheating dreams.

People who have been subverted consistently later have deceiving dreams. In case your lover has cheated beforehand, a cheating dream may show that you actually can't change the trust. If someone else has subverted you, you may be troubled your lover will do moreover.

While one swindling dream may not be a sign of an issue, in case you keep having them it'll be advocated, notwithstanding regardless of the difficulty to set the push to consider the impact cheating has had on your life, and put aside the push to filter through it.

The dream fills in as a course for your psyche to suss it immovable. Whether or not you're just inclination cheated out of their time, this sort of dream normally is certainly not far behind.

You Feel Betrayed

In case you keep having beguiling dreams, you might've starting late had a fight with your lover that made you feel deceived, if not in the ordinary sense. You may feel, for example, that you disagreed or that they weren't sorting out you. This betraying will ascend to the top in your dreams.

You Actually Suspect They're Cheating

Okay, so now for the terrible part: Sometimes, misleading dreams exhibit a subconscious conviction that your associate really could be cheating. Maybe you've dismissed the signs of cheating like the truth they're hiding their phone, changing their appearance, less motivated by sex, etc.

Considering the way that you would lean toward not to stand up to them in your insightful presence, yet it's harder to cover your suppositions when you're resting.

You Feel Like They Don't Care About Any of This

Many deceiving dreams, like the one I starting late, had, remember an astonishing absence of worry for the accessory's part. Consistently, the scalawag's hoodwinking legitimately out in the open. Moreover, he presumably reflects your accessory's nonappearance of care or stress that they're hurting you in one way or another or another, she says.

You may feel like they're not perceiving the torture they're causing. Assuming this is the case, the dream may be a call to push toward them with the objective that they can be more aware of how their direct is impacting you and the relationship.

Whatever the significance of the dream, it might be a cordial trade to inspect issues in your relationship, so consider granting it to your lover. Regardless, if it's in any capacity like mine, you can get a better than average laugh consequently.

CHAPTER SIX

THINGS PEOPLE SAY IF THEY WANT TO CHEAT

Scarcely people go into a relationship with the express desire for submitting untrustworthiness. Regardless, the startling truth is that cheating is unquestionably a reality for terribly various couples. In reality, about 16 percent of married women and men admit to having been shifty.

Anyway, what might you have the option to do to keep away from having your heart broken? In light of everything, the underlying advance is learning the signs that your accessory is on any occasion mulling over sabotaging you.

For instance, you'll be mindful if they're getting unnecessarily curious about when you'll be home.

Furthermore, if they really get some data about your insights on cheating, then you understand unfaithfulness is at the cutting edge of their considerations. Here are some indications from relationship authorities on some ordinary things people will say if they have to cheat (or if they starting at now are).

However, in the event that you're focused on that your relationship is falling to pieces, endeavor these Marriage Tips from Couples Who've Been Married for 50 Years.

Energetic couple with relationship issues fighting in the aft guest plan of a vehicle

If your lover really says something like this, by then you should consider that it's something they're genuinely contemplating doing, or if nothing else that they're troubled in the relationship at present.

Besides, it's not just another hairdo you should save watch for. Any gigantic changes in appearance, for example, "getting fit as a fiddle, or starting to wear beauty care products even more habitually," could be subtle signs of cheating. Besides, if you have to safeguard your relationship, Here's How to Spice Up Your Relationship.

Oh, John? I have no idea where he is.

colleagues having a dispute on the parlor seat things you should never say to a lone parent.

A person in a genuine relationship should have the alternative to uncover to you where their lover is where they aren't with them. In any case, someone who's almost cheating (deliberately or something different) will stop checking in with their mate or tremendous other, if just to endeavor to ignore that they have one regardless.

Woman hollering at her darling in the kitchen, signs of cheating.

Regardless of the way that the lover cheating (or examining cheating) is misguided, they are often in like manner the one in the relationship endeavoring to cut their associate down due to their own fault over their contemplations and extra exercises.

Work was fine."

A little bit at a time heading to isolate your marriage

Precisely when a relationship isn't working out, you may locate your partner is offering less and less to you. And for approaches to manage to uphold the closeness that once existed.

Consuming life accomplice

From time to time do partners have a reasonable and real discussion about accurately what practices they consider to be tricky and that unexpectedly prompts circumstantial cheating," says Solomon. Obviously, this doesn't have any significant bearing to cheating in the standard sense, yet suggests more to excited cheating or outperforming the limit among association and something other than what's expected. In the event that you need your partner to remain dedicated, it is vital that you plunk down with them and explain irrefutably what "cheating" incorporates.

The lady taking a gander at the telephone, things not to state to client maintain

Two or three companions basically need to know when their better half or buddy is getting back home since they miss them and can scarcely hold on to see them. Less great mates, regardless, could be checking considering the way that they need to know how much time they need to sneak around, or to investigate being with another person through dating applications or online visit rooms.

In the event that your loved one is intending to upgrade things up in the room, it could be a sign that they discover the current condition to be foreboding and disallowed. Likewise, recollecting that it's acceptable that they're despite all that trying to spare the relationship you have, this could besides be an indication that your associate is examining discovering fulfillment somewhere else. Besides, for additionally hypnotizing dating bearing, search after our reliable declaration.

More arranged white ladies couple strolling and grinning outside

Once more, your embellishment trying new things in bed isn't commonly a terrible thing. Notwithstanding, in the event that they're unexpectedly appearing in the stay with moves you've never watched, you may need to address what or who is giving them these insights.

CHAPTER SEVEN

HANDLING A CHEATING PARTNER

Being undermined is a dreadful inclination, however how you handle it can have a major part in your recovery cycle. Regardless of whether you attempt to remake the relationship or you choose to end things, figure out how you can mend and proceed forward. Here are some ways you can handle a cheating partner.

RESTORING TRUST

Choose if you need to restore trust. At the point when a partner is untrustworthy, it is a genuine break of trust. Furthermore, it is something that may demonstrate that this individual isn't commendable or prepared for a solid relationship.

On one hand, great individuals settle on awful decisions, and on the off chance that they are really grieved and can present appropriate reparations, pardoning a cheat can surprisingly make your relationship a better one, in the event that you basically can't believe that individual once more, the relationship is successfully dead.

Some key interesting points are:

Is your partner really heartbroken?

Did they deliberately let you know, or did you discover from another person?

Has such conduct occurred previously, or has the person in question vowed to not do it, and it has proceeded or deteriorated?

Is this aspect of a bigger image of helpless conduct towards you?

Do you believe you need to confide in this individual once more?

There is no set-in-stone response for this. This is totally up to the individual who has been undermined. It doesn't make a difference if the individual who has cheated is heartbroken, offered some kind of reparation, this can be a major issue straightforward.

Sentiments may change with time and further involvement in the bamboozling accomplice. It can go one way or the other, this is normal.

Good-natured companions and family members might need to offer basic guidance to make a brisk, conclusive choice. Know that you don't need to settle on a choice immediately by and large. It is your life.

Try to comprehend the idea of your accomplice's cheating. Individuals cheat for various reasons and it isn't generally about sex. Here and there individuals cheat since they are looking for an enthusiastic association, attempting to manage a misfortune or emergency, or looking for a getaway. This isn't a reason or explanation behind the conduct, nonetheless.

Discover why they cheated before you push ahead. If you don't mind be straightforward with me and mention to me what occurred." Know that they may not so much know why the treachery occurred. They may not so much have profoundly pondered it, or regardless of whether they did, they despite everything may not so much know why.

Furthermore, there might be reasons not completely comprehended by the individual. This doesn't pardon it, however, acknowledge "I don't have the foggiest idea" might be the genuine answer.

Some regular reasons include:

Appreciation for an alternate individual.

A craving for consideration, energy, or curiosity.

A disturbed marriage: lack of proper interaction between the both parties, worry in the marriage, accomplices becoming separated. It may also be born out of parenting and up binging defaults. In the event that the individual's parent was untrustworthy (particularly a similar sex).

The individual originates from a culture or subculture that expects and endures betrayal.

Psychological instability or issues. Individuals who cheat are not intellectually sick, however psychological maladjustment, for example, bipolar turmoil, sadness, or even lack of ability to concentrate consistently confusion would all be able to add to the helpless dynamic.

A solicitation that your accomplice removes all correspondence with the outsider. The third (or even fourth or fifth) party should be good and go for the relationship to endure.

You should request that your accomplice break all binds with the individual he had the affair with in the past and possibly any other individual that is giving your partner a positive signal that might give your relationship breakdown.

This cutting off might be troublesome if the outsider is a collaborator or another person that your accomplice sees consistently. This may require an adjustment in way of life, for example, leaving a place of employment, the softball crew, or moving to another town.

In the event that your accomplice is reluctant to cut off contact with the outsider, it might be an indication that they are reluctant to quit cheating. For this situation, you will most likely be unable to fix the relationship.

On the off chance that the outsider keeps on pursuing your accomplice regardless of being cut off, you and your accomplice might need to seek after a controlling request to get this individual far from you both.

Speak with your accomplice when you are prepared. Discovering that your accomplice has had an illicit relationship is likely reason you encounter a significant level of enthusiastic trouble.

You may require some time before you can converse with your accomplice about what occurred. It is essential to talk about the issue so as to push ahead in your relationship, however, don't feel like you have to examine the illicit relationship with your accomplice immediately. Take as much time as is needed and talk about it when you feel ready.

On the off chance that your accomplice compels you to talk, say something like, "I welcome that you need to talk, yet I am simply too harmed currently to discuss what occurred. It would be ideal if you show your adoration for me by giving me existence."

It is acceptable to be extremely, irate. You reserve each privilege to be harmed, irate, and in any case angry. Communicating this could sound not that pleasant but I believe your accomplice has to know how their activities has influenced you.

Not being straightforward and open about this implies they don't need to confront the truth of what has been done, and you may collapse in the event that you attempt to crush these regular and ordinary emotions. In the event that they attempt to stay away from or accuse you, this is an indication that they are not really tolerating.

Set cutoff networks about associations outside of your relationship. Endeavors for the most part happen when sound relationship limits are not respected. You save every extraordinary circumstance to explain what these are, whether or not the other individual gives reasons or "reasons" for the endeavor.

For example, your partner should not converse with a work accessory about you or your own issues. You and your advancement can share to coordinate a diagram of subjects that are satisfactory relatively as focuses that are not guarding conversations with embellishments and accomplices.

There should be no one-on-one trips with any person that has had an affair with your partner, because when this happen you will begin to feel that pain once more, as a matter of fact it will look like he or she just cheated once more. This include anyone that is still showing interest in dating your partner. When your partner can make this sacrifice you know he or she is ready to make amends, this can connect the re-trusting steps together gradually.

In other to reestablish trust, your accomplice should accept that they have lost your trust. Along these lines, you should know where your extra is obvious. This may have all the stores of being over the top to your frill, yet it is principal if they are spun around recuperating your trust.

Take alert not to cross into being implying or controlling while at the same time doing this. It's fine to check with your accessory about where they are, notwithstanding, it's not productive to flood them with works or calls, nor is it okay to offer them or the relationship if they don't react immediately. It's reasonable to be deficient.

A conversation about your partner's cheating, yet set cutoff communities. You, as the sold-out hoarding, find the opportunity to pick your cutoff communities and what you have to know and when.

Another idea is to plan two brief social events dependably to visit with your accomplice about the issue, as opposed to spreading the request constantly.

Set forth an endeavor not to demand that your accomplice reveal things that will be ludicrously horrendous for you to hear. You pick at whatever point and if you need certain information. You guarantee all ability to not fathom things too.

Your partner may be assuaging and restless for you to impart that you pardon them, at that point. Regardless, certified pardoning and recovery will likely require a tremendous undertaking. In like way, there is no game-plan for that.

The person who hoodwinked must fathom that they don't extra the decision to encourage when the fixing happens. It is okay if you need a more vital chance to recover before you pardon your partner.

To empower your partner to fathom, let them grasp that you are still too hurt to even consider evening consider exonerating in the long run and that you need additional time.

State something like, "I respect your appeasing choices and I need you to keep saying 'sorry' yet I am fundamentally not set up to excuse you yet."

It is OK to not exonerate. Cheating is an immense physical issue, and an aspect of the time is dangerous to a relationship. This doesn't usually mean you are not a fair or flawless individual or despite not with respect to enough. It is OK to state you have had enough.

Dealing with a misleading embellishment in the partition is unsafe. It is irrationally hard for you and your accomplice to work through this cycle separated, search for the help of a certified control who has significant consideration with individual issues. A marriage tutor can help you in dealing with your presumptions and have all the more consistent conversations.

Recall that marriage coaching won't offer a second course of action. Reestablishing trust in your relationship will require a critical venture.

Marriage or couples coaching can moreover help make removing the affiliation smoother. Despite the way that consultants will by and large endeavor to fix associations, they can empower the individuals to see when it isn't working, and how to push ahead toward that way as well.

CHAPTER EIGHT

BUILDING A BETTER RELATIONSHIP

Ranting a more noteworthy measure of your sentiments to your partner and asking your associate to do in like manner with you will help fortify your bond. Make it an affinity to trust in each other reliably. Some underlying requests for confiding in your lover include:

Recall when we used to go walking and talking around the zone, walking the canines together? We ought to do that tonight. What do you think?

What happened yesterday between us turned out ineffectively, and I have to think of another way this time I will take some full breaths and listen even more industriously.

To push ahead in your relationship, you will both need to make sense of how to see each other's needs. The best way to deal with uncovering what your associate needs, and let them perceive what you need, is to examine it.

If you don't have a clue what your life accomplice needs or needs, the best way to deal with find is to present requests and tune in. If you in spite of everything you still don't have a clue, present more requests by asking, like I will always recommend communication is the best form of knowing anyone, try to ask good questions that is orientated in a presentable manner.

Exhibiting appreciation through evident honors is a huge part of a strong relationship.

Guarantee that you and your partner think about the hugeness of applauding each other and that you both are skilled to do it well. Incredible honors should not solely be certified and unequivocal, they should moreover be communicated as an "I" declaration rather than as a ""you" proclamation.

For example, if your associate cleans the kitchen, don't state "You made a tolerable appearing of cleaning the kitchen." Instead, state "I esteem that you cleaned the kitchen." Using I as opposed to you tell your partner how you feel, not just that you observed.

A solicitation that your lover sets out to change. If you presume that you are set up to push ahead in your relationship with your accessory, you should demand that your associate assure you that they won't follow a comparable case which directed your relationship to the previous provocation.

Develop results to deal with the opportunity of another endeavor. Since there is a probability that your accessory may swindle again, you ought to participate to develop repercussions for another issue.

These outcomes may fuse things like partition or various repercussions. You may need to get these results recorded as a printed copy and work with a lawful guide to make them really official.

Acknowledge when to remove the affiliation. In case things don't improve despite the aggregate of your sincere endeavors and the help of marriage coaching, you may need to recognize that the relationship can't be fixed.

SIGNS THAT THE RELATIONSHIP MAY BE UNRECOVERABLE INCLUDE:

Steady combating, both parties are still engaging in physical combat, they are not taking things easy with themselves, they still go on serious battle because of little misunderstanding, it will be better if they both go their separate ways.

Inability to interface with your lover.

Inability to identify with or get compassion from your lover.

Hurt and shock that doesn't fade away with time.

Inability to pardon your lover's shortcomings or deficiencies.

CHAPTER NINE

MOVING FORWARD

Here's what to do moving forward.

The disclosure that one extra has been precarious to the going with can be beaten to a relationship, at any rate, it doesn't regularly mean its culmination.

The central advancement is to permit your emotions to pass, the disappointment, the tendencies of wrong conduct. Give yourself the presence to feel what you need to feel without making any genuine decisions.

There is no inspiration to shape an amazing additional piece around urges that may prop up for only a short period of time. You would uphold not to live in mourn simply considering the way that you acted absurdly energetic.

A few signs on getting over these feelings include:

Mourn in case you need to lament; shut if you have to a shut-in. Set forth an endeavor not to attempt to skirt this turn of events, or it will tail you for an astonishing additional part.

Think about you, explicitly:

Many people will say, "Think about the children." But enough examinations have found that youngsters from dismal homes can twist up likewise as hurt and hurt as the group of isolated gatekeepers. Your ability to raise your children and give the best characteristics to them will depend on your psychological quality and your happiness, corresponding to your accomplice. Think about you: what do you need?

Make an effort not to transform into your sharpness:

Grieving is critical, anyway, it's not your character. Make an effort not to let alcohol or drugs or whatever else you do to numb the anguish accept power over your life.

There was a part of your life before your associate, and there will be significant for your life after this event, whether or not you choose to stay together or not. Keep yourself grounded, for your future.

Search for coordinating or treatment social occasions:

Don't be humiliated if you think you need help. If your

friends and family aren't adequate, then find something other than what's expected. A consideration gathering can do contemplates for someone who feels lost, alone, and bewildered, because they help you with the understanding that what you are encountering is a cycle, as you see them at various steps of the cycle.

At the point when the hidden surge of emotions has spent, it's an ideal chance to plunk down and think, both with and without your lover. Understand why your associate cheated.

There will be different reasons, certainly, notwithstanding, both you and your lover must hope to address the request, you might want to continue with the relationship.

In case you want to continue with the relationship, recognize what necessities to change to shield this level of unfairness from happening again, whether or not that suggests improving the way in which you act, changing your practices in the room, disengaging power even more comparable in the relationship, or considering changes to your opinion of agreeable in your association.

You will find that all around, deceiving mates regularly still should be in the relationship, just a few noteworthy adjustments ought to be made.

Remember life can go on anyway just if you choose to make it go. Understanding why your lover cheated might be the best learning experience you will really have.

Directions to save your relationship

First and foremost, we should make one thing comprehended, because your lover is showing a couple of the practices that I just talked about don't suggest that they're obviously cheating. It may very well be that these are pointers of trouble ahead in your relationship.

Notwithstanding, if you've seen a couple of these pointers in your associate starting late, and you're feeling that things aren't on track with your relationship, I ask you to act to get something going now before issues crumble.

Various things can bit by bit pollute a relationship partition, nonappearance of correspondence, and sexual issues. If not oversaw successfully, these issues can metamorphosize into foul play and disconnectedness.